Portscatho

The Pandora Inn, Restronguet

ST. MAWES, ROSELAND
AND THE FAL ESTUARY

A pictorial souvenir

SALMON

INTRODUCTION

The delightful Fal estuary and Roseland Peninsula on Cornwall's south coast is one of the most picturesque and unspoilt parts of the British Isles. Seeming to stand apart from the rest of Cornwall, this serene and lovely area is threaded through with rivers and wooded, tidal creeks where villages and hamlets have for centuries depended on boats and the sea. As well as a number of delightful small fishing harbours, beautiful beaches, cliff scenery and lush, green countryside, the Roseland Peninsula includes the dignified little resort of St. Mawes. From its position on the eastern bank of the River Fal, which winds inland towards the county town of Truro, this attractive waterside village looks out across the estuary towards the maritime town of Falmouth. On Roseland, each pretty village and hamlet has its own individual charm and here, in village streets and public gardens alike, exotic species of trees and plants flourish whilst, along the banks of the Fal estuary, tree-lined creeks and inlets harbour ancient inns and hamlets. There are lovely walks through ancient woodland or along the seashore, and when the holiday-makers and visiting yachtsmen have gone, it is possible to enjoy the rich wildlife where curlew, oystercatcher and heron are among the resident birds. Artists and photographers have long been attracted to Roseland and the River Fal, where the variety of its scenic beauty is unmatched, even in a county as stunningly beautiful as Cornwall.

Sunset at St. Mawes

ST. MAWES

Situated between Carrick Roads and the Percuil River at the end of the Roseland Peninsula, the popular little resort of St. Mawes is very much a seafaring community. Built on terraces and well protected both from the north and the south, it enjoys the mild climate which has justly earned this part of the coast the title of Cornish Riviera. A popular centre for boating activities of all kinds, the quayside is always a lively scene with yachts and other small boats coming and going, including the ferry which plies across the Fal estuary linking St. Mawes with the busy port of Falmouth. St. Mawes is a village of narrow lanes and quaint corners. Victory Hill lies in the centre of the ancient

fishing village and at the top, housed in a stone building which dates back over 600 years, is a Holy Well associated with the Celtic Saint Maudez, from whom the village took its name. The sheltered harbour and small sandy beaches are overlooked by St. Mawes Castle, built by Henry VIII as part of his coastal defences against a possible invasion from the Continent. More highly decorated than any of Henry's other coastal forts, it is an outstanding example of Tudor military architecture with a fine keep shaped like a clover leaf with three huge

St. Mawes Harbour

Victory Hill, St. Mawes

circular bastions. Situated at the end of the peninsula, St. Anthony Head offers superb views across Falmouth Bay. A coal beacon once burned here, but in 1835 the present lighthouse was completed. Perched 65 feet above the sea it marks the entrance to the Carrick Roads and warns ships away from the infamous Manacles Rocks. Until 1954 it possessed a huge bell which hung outside the tower and functioned as a fog signal. In that year the lighthouse was connected to mains electricity and the bell was replaced by a modern fog-horn. Roseland's mild climate enables a wide variety of plants to flourish here in both private and public gardens. Palms and other subtropical plants abound at Lamorran House, a hillside garden in the Mediterranean tradition. It is divided into a number of intimate areas with unusual plants and interesting combinations of colour and foliage as well as pools, streams and a Japanese water garden.

The Quay, St. Mawes

12   A still morning at St. Mawes

Traditional boat racing in Falmouth Week   13

14   A summer's day at Castle Beach in St. Mawes

St. Mawes Castle was built by Henry VIII to protect the approach to Carrick Roads   15

A peaceful evening at St. Mawes

The Italianate gardens at Lamorran House contain a profusion of subtropical plants   19

20   A beautiful coastal walk leads from St. Mawes to St. Anthony Head

Built in 1835, St. Anthony Head light is visible from 22 nautical miles distance   21

ROSELAND

The beautiful and unspoilt Roseland Peninsula extends from the River Fal in the west to Gerrans Bay in the east and, in addition to the delightful resort of St. Mawes, it includes a number of picturesque villages. St. Just-in-Roseland provides a peaceful contrast with the busy port of Falmouth on the other side of the river. Nestling at the water's edge overlooking St. Just Creek, the pretty little church was built in 1261. The village of Philleigh once stood on the main road from London to Land's End, but today this charming little spot with its

16th century Roseland Inn seems miles away from the bustle of modern life. At nearby Tolverne, in beautiful surroundings on a tranquil stretch of the River Fal, Smugglers Cottage is a picturesque thatched 15th century cottage and tea-rooms. Portscatho was once a quiet fishing village and, with its narrow streets and tiny harbour, it still retains a tranquil atmosphere, although the boats which crowd into the harbour today are mainly used for pleasure. Facing east across Gerrans Bay, Portscatho offers magnificent views towards Nare Head and the isolated stack known as Gull Rock which provides a nesting place for many species of sea bird. Lying in a sheltered position

St. Just-in-Roseland Church

The Creek, St. Just-in-Roseland

in a well-wooded valley, the delightful village of Veryan is known for its unusual Round Houses with their thatched roofs surmounted by a cross. Legend has it that they were built for the five daughters of the vicar and they were round in shape so that there were no corners in which the devil could hide. An unspoiled country pub, the 16th century New Inn lies in the heart of this historic village. One of Cornwall's many diminutive ports and harbours, Portloe nestles in a steep valley down which a stream runs into the narrow rocky cove where the slipway is still used by fishermen. Built in the early 1800s, Caerhays Castle occupies a dramatic site above Porthluney Cove. The gardens were extensively developed later in the century when the owners took advantage of several plant-hunting expeditions to import vast quantities of exotic species which now grow amongst native plants such as bluebells, wild garlic and some exceptional old beech trees.

St. Just-in-Roseland   25

26   The Smugglers Cottage at Tolverne is a delightful stop-off for river trips up the River Fal

The 16th century Roseland Inn at Philleigh nestles in a delightful rural setting

Low tide at Portscatho

Portscatho

Cottages cling to the shoreline in the picturesque seaside village of Portscatho 31

32   Portscatho's tiny harbour overlooks the wide sweep of Gerrans Bay

Nare Head is the backdrop to beautiful Pendower Beach   33

34 Nare Head lies amid spectacular coastal scenery

Gerrans Bay from Nare Head

36   The traditional 16th century New Inn at Veryan

Built in the 19th century, the circular cottages are a unique feature of Veryan   37

Portloe

FH75

FY 180

FY 66

The unspoiled fishing village of Portloe is a cluster of cottages around a rocky cove   39

42 Caerhays Castle is one of the finest woodland gardens in the country

A carpet of daffodils provide a splash of spring colour at Caerhays

THE RIVER FAL

Surrounded by scenery of the utmost beauty, the River Fal flows between wooded banks with countless delightful creeks leading off to right and left. The ancient ferry crossing on King Harry Reach, named after Henry VI who swam the river here on horseback, is set on one of the most beautiful stretches of the river. At the head of the estuary the gardens of Trelissick House are favoured by the Gulf Stream and a warm climate. They offer a wonderful mixture of natural woodland and rare shrubs and plants, including ferns, bamboos and other moisture-loving plants. A number of delightful little hamlets lie on the many wooded creeks and inlets between Falmouth and Truro, among them the pretty villages of Feock and Mylor. The picturesque Pandora Inn on Restronguet Creek dates in part from the 13th century when it was called the Passage House. Its name was changed in memory of the *Pandora*, a naval ship which sank in 1791. Now a popular holiday centre, Falmouth has been a flourishing port for over 200 years and has one of the finest natural

44   Dawn light on the Fal

Reflections on the Fal

King Harry Ferry

harbours in the world. The old town is centred around 17th century Custom House Quay, where excise officers used to burn contraband tobacco in a furnace which can still be seen. Backed by wooded hills, Falmouth is situated on a superb bay and has several popular beaches. Located on the waterfront, the National Maritime Museum comprises a number of galleries with displays relating to boats and the sea, including the stories of some famous craft, navigation and meteorology, boat building and the Cornish maritime heritage. Guarding the Carrick Roads at the entrance to the river, Pendennis Castle offers superb coastal views. Flushing, on the other side of the creek, was once a thriving port trading with the West Indies and America, but today its little harbour is mainly used for recreation.

Cottage at Trelissick 47

48   There are delightful vistas over the River Fal from Trelissick Gardens

Trelissick Gardens are set in more than 400 acres of magnificent parkland

50   Pretty little Feock takes its name from little-known Cornish saint, Fioc

Sheltered Mylor is a mecca for yatchsmen and boaters 51

The 13th century Pandora Inn at Restronguet lies in a beautiful waterside setting

54   Flushing is a picturesque fishing village across the water from Falmouth

Boats lie at their moorings at Custom House Quay in Falmouth

56   Evening sunshine at Falmouth

The National Maritime Museum at Falmouth houses a fascinating collection of small craft

Flushing from Falmouth

60 Falmouth is reputed to be the world's third largest natural harbour

Pendennis Castle has defended Carrick Roads from Tudor times to the modern day

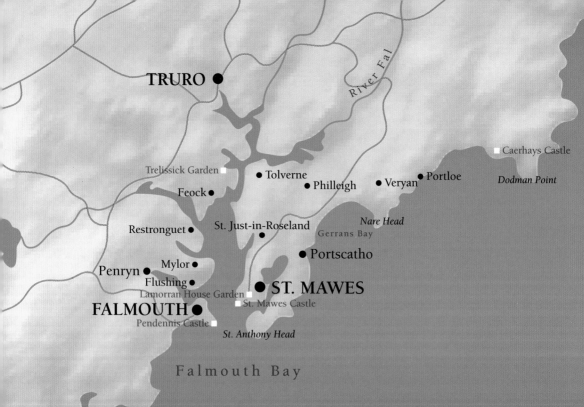

Low tide at Penryn Creek

Printed and published by J. Salmon Ltd., 100 London Road, Sevenoaks, Kent.
Telephone: 01732 452381   Email: enquiries@jsalmon.co.uk   Website: www.jsalmon.com
ISBN 1 84640 092 9
Photographs by Chris Wormald

Product code: 12-08-44-02

Front cover picture: St. Mawes Harbour   Back cover picture: Reflections on the Fal

Penryn Creek